NEAR ONE CATTAIL

Turtles, Logs and Leaping Frogs

By Anthony D. Fredericks

Illustrated by Jennifer DiRubbio

Dawn Publications

*For the faculty, staff and students at Lake Murray Elementary School
in Lexington, South Carolina, whose devotion to wetlands education
serves as a model of exemplary environmental awareness. — ADF*

*To my sons, Zachary & Jason:
My happiest moments are the times I spend with
the two of you. I love you both more than anything. — JDR*

Library of Congress Cataloging-in-Publication Data

Fredericks, Anthony D.
  Near one cattail : turtles, logs, and leaping frogs / by Anthony D. Fredericks ; illustrated by Jennifer DiRubbio.-- 1st ed.
     p. cm.
  ISBN 1-58469-070-4 (hardcover) -- ISBN 1-58469-071-2 (pbk.)
  1. Wetland animals--Juvenile literature. I. DiRubbio, Jennifer, ill. II. Title.
  QL113.8.F74 2005
  591.768--dc22
                          2004018958

Dawn Publications
12402 Bitney Springs Road
Nevada City, CA 95959
530-274-7775
nature@dawnpub.com

Printed in China

10 9 8 7 6 5 4 3 2 1
First Edition

Design and computer production by Patty Arnold, Menagerie Design and Publishing

Dear Friends:

Paddle on over and let me introduce you to my neighborhood. Things are really hopping here! Get it? This is a wetland. Now, you may think that a wetland is just one big swamp...and you'd almost be right. But you should also know that a wetland is a wild and oozy place to live for many critters.

A wetland is a vacation spot for migrating birds—a place to rest when they travel to and from their winter or summer homes. It's also a nursery for small fish and other creatures that need a safe environment in which to grow up. Wetlands control floods and help protect water supplies from pollutants and other impurities. And, if you look closely you might just see all my tadpole babies swimming around. Ribbit! Ribbit!

But our wetland home is in danger. Many of the bogs, swamps, marshes and other wet and soggy places in this country are disappearing. That's because some people want to build more houses, highways or shopping centers. There are even folks who just don't like marshy, soggy places. So, many wetland areas are being filled, dredged and drained. We need your help. Wetlands are full of more life than you might see anywhere else. Saving them means protecting the homes of many plants and many animals.

I hope you enjoy your visit to my buggy, muggy home! So, come along and "log on" to some great adventures and incredible discoveries.

Your big-eyed buddy,

Frog

Here is a world where tadpoles play,
    And crowds of bugs dance through the day,
With lilies and duckweed everywhere,
    Some long-legged birds and a crayfish pair.
Among the rushes where herons repose
    A fuzzy cattail flowers and grows.

This is the **cattail**.

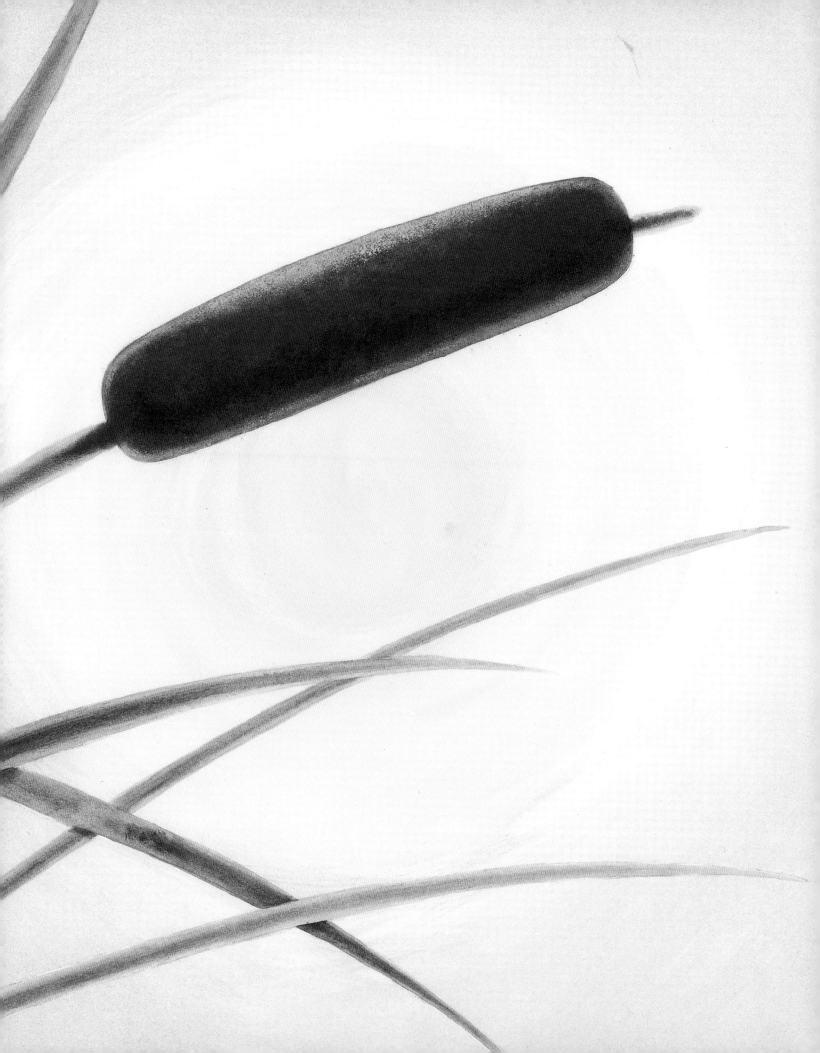

The marshy land with a layer of ooze
  Was explored by a girl in high-topped shoes.
A quizzical thought crossed her face:
  "What creatures live in this bog-boggy place?"

When she looked at the wildlife one by one,
  As they skittered and scattered in the noonday sun,
She discovered a kingdom wild and grand,
  A web of life in a soggy land.

These are the **frogs** with big bulging eyes,
Who whip out their tongues to capture some flies,
Within a rich land, all swampy and green,
Creatures abound in this waterlogged scene!

Sunbathing **turtles** on a moss-covered log
Bask in the warmth of this mug-muggy bog,
Neighbors to frogs with big bulging eyes,
Who whip out their tongues to capture some flies,
Within a rich land, all swampy and green,
Creatures abound in this waterlogged scene!

A zip-zipping **dragonfly** skitters all day,
  Hunting mosquitoes and other small prey,
Past sunbathing turtles on a moss-covered log
  Who bask in the warmth of this mug-muggy bog,
Neighbors to frogs with big bulging eyes,
  Who whip out their tongues to capture some flies,
Within a rich land, all swampy and green,
  Creatures abound in this waterlogged scene!

Brown-feathered **ducks** with paddling feet
   Poke near the shore for some food they can eat.
A zip-zipping dragonfly skitters all day,
   Hunting mosquitoes and other small prey,
Past sunbathing turtles on a moss-covered log
   Who bask in the warmth of this mug-muggy bog,
Neighbors to frogs with big bulging eyes,
   Who whip out their tongues to capture some flies,
Within a rich land, all swampy and green,
   Creatures abound in this waterlogged scene!

This is the **muskrat** with a round furry head,
  Asleep in her lodge on a dry grassy bed,
While brown-feathered ducks with paddling feet
  Poke near the shore for some food they can eat.
A zip-zipping dragonfly skitters all day,
  Hunting mosquitoes and other small prey,
Past sunbathing turtles on a moss-covered log
  Who bask in the warmth of this mug-muggy bog,
Neighbors to frogs with big bulging eyes,
  Who whip out their tongues to capture some flies,
Within a rich land, all swampy and green,
  Creatures abound in this waterlogged scene!

A paddling **beetle** with legs long and brown
  Scoots over the water, on its back—upside down!
Close to the muskrat with a round furry head,
  Who sleeps in her lodge on a dry grassy bed,
While brown-feathered ducks with paddling feet
  Poke near the shore for some food they can eat.
A zip-zipping dragonfly skitters all day,
  Hunting mosquitoes and other small prey,
Past sunbathing turtles on a moss-covered log
  Who bask in the warmth of this mug-muggy bog,
Neighbors to frogs with big bulging eyes,
  Who whip out their tongues to capture some flies,
Within a rich land, all swampy and green,
  Creatures abound in this waterlogged scene!

A sunbathing **snake** lies curled in the heat,
  Then slips underwater for fish it can eat,
Near a paddling beetle with legs long and brown
  Who scoots over water, on its back—upside down!
Close to the muskrat with a round furry head,
  Who sleeps in her lodge on a dry grassy bed,
While brown-feathered ducks with paddling feet
  Poke near the shore for some food they can eat.
A zip-zipping dragonfly skitters all day,
  Hunting mosquitoes and other small prey,
Past sunbathing turtles on a moss-covered log
  Who bask in the warmth of this mug-muggy bog,
Neighbors to frogs with big bulging eyes,
  Who whip out their tongues to capture some flies,
Within a rich land, all swampy and green,
  Creatures abound in this waterlogged scene!

Here's a medley of critters who swim, soar or crawl
In this sog-soggy home that protects one and all.
It's a marvelous place to explore and observe—
A grand web of life to cherish and preserve.

Field Notes

Hundreds of plants and animals can be found in freshwater wetlands throughout North America. The specific species described and illustrated in this book can be found in the marshes, swamps, prairie potholes and bogs that make up 90 percent of the wetlands in the United States. Many animals are permanent residents; others are visitors—those who come and go depending on the season and the amount of available water.

Cattails

Cattails have been around since the time of the dinosaurs and are the most familiar of all wetland plants. Their swaying brown clusters can be seen at the edges of marshes, swamps, or wherever there is shallow, standing water for part of the year. Some species grow to be over twelve feet tall. Each cattail possesses thousands of tiny flowers tightly compressed into a compact mass on the top of their stems. During late summer and early fall, these structures begin to come apart, releasing their seeds into the wind.

Fantastic Fact: Native Americans used cattails as a source of food, as a medicine, to make baskets and mats, and to thatch roofs.

Frogs

Frogs are common wetland creatures. They usually live along the edge of standing or open water. If a frog senses danger it hops into the water and swims away. Adult frogs eat insects, spiders and small crustaceans. After mating, a female frog will often lay large clutches of eggs—as many as 20,000 at one time. Eggs hatch within a month and the tiny tadpoles will feed on algae. As they grow larger, tadpoles eat tiny insects and other small wetland creatures. They change into frogs six to 24 months later.

Fantastic Fact: The largest frog in the world is the Goliath Frog which has a body length of more than 13 inches. That's bigger than a dinner plate.

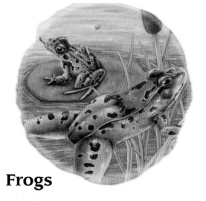

Turtles

There are 48 species of turtles that live in the United States. Turtles can be found in a variety of aquatic environments such as wetlands. Unlike other reptiles, turtles have expanded ribs that are incorporated into a protective shell. They also have a horny beak instead of teeth. Turtles are egg-layers and typically lay two to three eggs at a time (with the exception of some sea turtles). The Painted Turtle is the most widespread turtle in North America. It enjoys sunning itself on fallen logs and several may be found on a single log at the same time.

Fantastic Fact: The first turtles appeared on the earth about 200 million years ago—long before the dinosaurs.

Dragonflies

Dragonfly nymphs emerge from eggs laid under the water. The nymphs may live underwater for up to five years. Then they climb up a plant, shed their skin, dry their wings in the sun and swoop over the water. Although they are a common wetland creature, their average life expectancy is only four to six weeks. They are strong fliers; some species are even migratory, traveling long distances between wetland areas. When resting, dragonflies (unlike damselflies) hold their wings open. When in flight they are usually hunting for mosquitoes, tadpoles or small insects to eat. Their chief predators are frogs and fish.

Fantastic Fact: The compound eyes of some species of dragonfly are so close together they sometimes meet on the top of the head.

Ruddy ducks are frequent wetland birds. They have a black and white head, a brown body and a black tail that is often held straight up. They build their nests with cattails, sedges and other grasses. These nests, which hold 6 to 20 eggs, are carefully hidden among the wetland plants. They feed on snails, tiny insects and various types of wetland plants.

Fantastic Fact: Males and females have bills that are black. However, during the mating season the male's bill often turns blue.

Ruddy Ducks

Muskrats are rodents (related to rats and mice) that can be found in most wetland areas. They are adapted to life in a watery world. They have partially webbed feet that help them swim. Their flattened tails are like rudders, guiding them through and around various wetland plants. Muskrats eat many varieties of plants, but depend primarily on cattail roots. They also use shredded cattails and other plants to build their lodges.

Fantastic Fact: Muskrats have two layers of fur—one short and thick and the other long. This provides the muskrat with a waterproof coat, keeping it warm and dry in water.

Muskrats

The backswimmer is a small insect, about one-half inch in length, that lives in wetlands around the world. Pale brown in color, the backswimmer has long back legs fringed with fine hairs. For much of the day a backswimmer rests upside down. When an enemy approaches, the backswimmer, still upside down, uses its hind legs as oars and quickly propels itself across the surface of the water. It also uses this form of locomotion to attack and eat mosquitoes, tadpoles and small fish.

Fantastic Fact: In winter, when water freezes, backswimmers walk around upside down under the ice.

Backswimmer

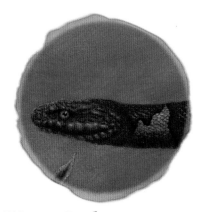

Water snakes can be found in many lakes, rivers, bogs, swamps, marshes and wetland areas throughout the United States from sea level up to 4,500 feet in elevation. One of the most well-known is the Northern Water Snake. This snake, like other freshwater snakes, basks on shoreline rocks or along the water's edge. It hunts frogs, small fish and salamanders. Its color ranges from reddish brown to brownish-black with a white, yellow or gray belly. It sometimes reaches a length of 4 1/2 feet.

Fantastic Fact: The Northern Water Snake has an anticoagulant in its saliva, just like many poisonous snakes. Its bite will cause a victim to bleed profusely. Although it is not venomous, it is often mistaken for dangerous snakes, such as the water moccasin.

Water Snakes

How to Learn More

Dear Reader,

Wetlands can be found in every state and every province in North America. Here are some of my favorite resources about wetlands and the animals that live in them.

Anthology for the Earth (1998) edited by Judy Allen, a wonderful collection of art, essays and poetry about the planet Earth.

Squishy, Misty, Damp & Muddy (1996) by Molly Cone, is an easy-to-read book for young naturalists filled with valuable information and engaging photographs.

Wading into Wetlands (1997) by the National Wildlife Federation, is a book chock full of activities and learning opportunities for students of all ages. It's a great resource.

Leapfrogging Through Wetlands (1998) by Margaret Anderson, Nancy Field and Karen Stephenson, is a delightful collection of information and colorful illustrations that presents the importance of wetlands for everyone.

America's Wetlands (1995) by Frank Staub, is an in-depth look at wetlands across the United States and why they are so valuable.

One Small Square: Swamp (1997) by Donald M. Silver is an incredible book overflowing with information, illustrations, and valuable facts about life in a swamp

Here are some of the other children's books I've written.

Amazing Animals (2000), profiles more than 60 fantastic creatures and incredible critters.

Around One Cactus: Owls, Bats and Leaping Rats (2003), a fun-filled book about the incredible variety of animal life that lives in and around a Saguaro cactus.

Clever Camouflagers (2000), an amazing book about the clever ways in which some animals hide from their predators.

In One Tidepool: Crabs, Snails and Salty Tails (2002), an engaging story about a young girl and her discoveries in a tidepool on a rocky shore.

Slugs (1999), offers young readers all they ever wanted to know about these amazing creatures.

Under One Rock: Bugs, Slugs and Other Ughs (2001), a rhythmic description of the colorful creatures that live together beneath a single rock.

Weird Walkers (2000), a book about a lizard that walks on water, a fish that walks on land, and an animal that walks upside down.

Zebras (2001), delightful information and eye-popping photographs about these wonderful creatures.

Here are the names and addresses of organizations working to protect and reclaim wetlands. You may want to contact them to find out what they are doing and how you can become involved.

Ducks Unlimited, Inc.
One Waterfowl Way
Memphis, TN 38120
www.ducks.org

National Audubon Society
700 Broadway
New York, NY 10003
www.audubon.org

Izaak Walton League of America
707 Conservation Lane
Gaithersburg, MD 20878
www.iwla.org

National Wildlife Federation
11100 Wildlife Center Drive
Reston, VA 20190
www.nwf.org

Wetlands International (Headquarters)
P.O. Box 471
6700 AL Wageningen
The Netherlands
www.wetlands.org

Wetlands International (North America)
c/o USFWS, Div. of International Affairs
4401 North Fairfax Drive
Room 730-ARLSQ
Arlington, VA 22203-1622

If you or your teacher would like to learn more about me and the books I write, please log on to my web site, www.afredericks.com.

Anthony D. Fredericks is a veteran nature explorer. He grew up on the beaches of southern California and during summers hiked the Sierra Nevada mountains of eastern California. Later he attended high school in the high desert region of Arizona where his love of desert life blossomed. While a student at the University of Arizona in Tucson he often spent his free time trekking through and exploring the Sonoran desert. Now Tony explores the mountainside in Pennsylvania where he and his wife live. A former classroom teacher and reading specialist, he is Professor of Education at York College. As the author of more than 25 children's books he is a frequent visitor to schools around the country, where he shares the wonders of nature with a new generation of naturalists.

Jennifer DiRubbio is both a passionate artist and an avid environmentalist. She has been active as an artist for several organizations that promote nature and a healthy planet. Jennifer graduated with a BFA from Pratt Institute in 1992. She keeps her home and studio in Merrick, New York, as "green" and environmentally sound as possible, where her husband and two young children also work and play.

OTHER BOOKS BY
ANTHONY FREDERICKS AND JENNIFER DiRUBBIO

Under One Rock: Bugs, Slugs and Other Ughs. A whole community of creatures lives under rocks. No child will be able to resist taking a peek after reading this.

In One Tidepool: Crabs, Snails and Salty Tails. Have you ever ventured to the edge of the sea and peered into a tidepool? A colorful community of creatures lives there!

Around One Cactus: Owls, Bats and Leaping Rats. A saguaro cactus may look lonely, standing in the dry, dry desert—but it is a haven for creatures, both cute and creepy!

A FEW OTHER NATURE AWARENESS TITLES FROM
DAWN PUBLICATIONS

Stickeen: John Muir and the Brave Little Dog by Donnell Rubay, illustrated by Christopher Canyon. This classic true story of John Muir's favorite wilderness adventure transformed the relationship between Muir and a dog.

Eliza and the Dragonfly by Susie Caldwell Rinehart, illustrated by Anisa Claire Hovemann. Almost despite herself, Eliza becomes entranced by the "awful" dragonfly nymph—and before long, both of them are transformed.

Earth Day, Birthday by Pattie Schnetzler, illustrated by Chad Wallace. To the tune of "The Twelve Days of Christmas," here is a sing-along, read-along book that honors the animals, the environment, and a universal holiday all in one fresh approach.

Sunshine On My Shoulders and Ancient Rhymes: A Dolphin Lullaby by John Denver, adapted and illustrated as picture books by Christopher Canyon, make John Denver's most child-friendly and nature-aware lyrics a delightful new experience. (The John Denver & Kids Series)

Dawn Publications is dedicated to inspiring in children a deeper understanding and appreciation for all life on Earth. Call 800-545-7475 or go online at www.dawnpub.com.